This Book Belongs to:

_____

Born on:

_____

BABY MEMORY BOOK:

Baby's First Five Years

All About You

[Baby's First Photo]

Baby's name: _____

Birth date: _____   Time born: _____

Birth weight: _____   Birth length: _____

Eye color: _____   Hair color: _____

Place of birth: _____

Person that delivered you: _____

Who was in the delivery room: _____

Others in attendance: _____

When labor started and how long it lasted: _____

How and why we chose your name: _____

What your name means: _____

Nicknames for baby: _____

Other names we considered: _____

Labor and delivery stories:

_____
_____
_____
_____
_____
_____
_____
_____
_____

Visitors and guests:

_____
_____
_____
_____
_____
_____
_____

Birth Announcement

Birth Certificate

Baby's Newborn Footprint

Date: Age:

Baby's Newborn Handprint

Date: Age:

Baby's 1 Year Old Footprint

Date:  Age:

Baby's 1 Year Old Handprint

Date: Age:

Pregnancy Time

How and when your mom found out she was pregnant:

_____

When we told people we were having a baby: _____

How we announced the pregnancy: _____

When we found out you were a boy or a girl: _____

When mom felt the first kick: _____

Mom's cravings during pregnancy: _____

Pregnancy pictures, memories, and stories: _____

_____

_____

_____

_____

_____

_____

_____

_____

_____

Your Ultrasound Pictures

Baby Shower

Date: _____

Location: _____

Who hosted the shower: _____

Those in attendance:

_____

_____

_____

_____

_____

Special gifts and memories:

_____

_____

_____

_____

_____

_____

_____

Baby Shower Photos and Memories

The World Around You

World leaders: _____

_____

Major news stories: _____

_____

_____

Popular songs, movies, television shows and celebrities:

_____

_____

Price of common items:

Gas: _____

Milk: _____

Loaf of bread: _____

Pack of diapers: _____

Movie ticket: _____

Postage stamp: _____

Your First Home

[photo]

Address: _____

When we brought you home: _____

Weather: _____

Your bedroom

[photo]

Your Firsts

First bath: _____

[photo]

First smile: _____   First laugh: _____

First time slept through the night: _____

First time rolled over: _____   First time sitting up: _____

First time standing alone: _____

First time crawled: _____   First time walked: _____

First solid foods: _____

First words: _____

Your Firsts

Date of first haircut: _____

Age: _____   Place: _____

[photo]

[attach small envelope to hold
snip of first haircut]

All About You

Your favorite foods: _____
_____

Your favorite songs: _____

Your favorite toys: _____

Your favorite books: _____
_____

Other favorites: _____
_____

Things you did not like: _____
_____
_____

Sleeping patterns: _____
_____

Daily activities: _____
_____
_____
_____

Playmates and friends: _____
_____

# See How You Grew

Your Baby Teeth

Date Appeared/Emerged

Age Typically Emerges

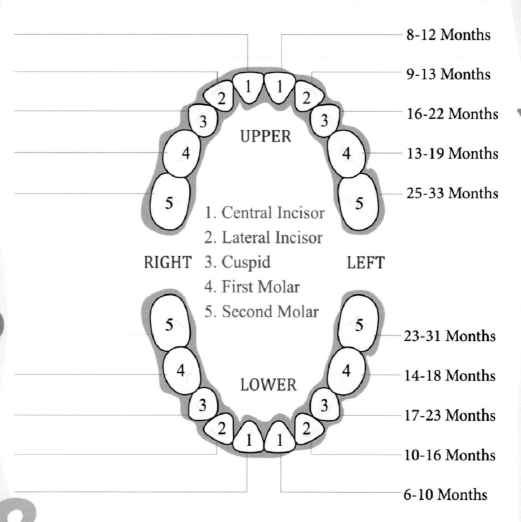

8-12 Months

9-13 Months

16-22 Months

13-19 Months

25-33 Months

UPPER

1. Central Incisor
2. Lateral Incisor
RIGHT   3. Cuspid   LEFT
4. First Molar
5. Second Molar

LOWER

23-31 Months

14-18 Months

17-23 Months

10-16 Months

6-10 Months

Family Tree

Great-grandmother
Great-grandfather
Great-grandmother
Great-grandfather
Great-grandmother
Great-grandfather
Great-grandmother
Great-grandfather

Grandmother
Grandfather
Grandmother
Grandfather

Mother
Father

Child

About Your Mother

Mother's name: _____

Where she was born: _____

When she was born: _____

Where she grew up: _____

Her brothers and sisters: _____

_____

Where she went to school: _____

Her occupation when you were born: _____

Her talents, hobbies, and general interests: _____

_____

_____

[Photo of your mother]

About Your Father

[Photo of your father]

Father's name: _____

Where he was born: _____

When he was born: _____

Where he grew up: _____

His brothers and sisters: _____

_____

Where he went to school: _____

His occupation when you were born: _____

His talents, hobbies, and general interests: _____

_____

Story of Your Mother and Father

How, when, and where we met:

_____
_____
_____
_____
_____
_____

Our story:

_____
_____
_____
_____
_____
_____
_____
_____
_____
_____
_____
_____
_____

Your Extended Family

Your brothers and sisters:

Aunts, uncles and cousins:

Your Day of Blessings

When: _____

Where: _____

Who was present: _____

_____

Thoughts and photos from this special day:

_____

_____

_____

_____

_____

_____

_____

_____

_____

_____

_____

_____

_____

_____

Holidays and Special Events

Holidays and Special Events

Holidays and Special Events

Baby Travels

Baby Travels

Photos of You and Your Family

Photos of You and Your Family

Letter from Mother

Letter from Father

My 1ˢᵗ Twelve Months

The Day of My Birth

Name _____

Weather ☁ _____

#1 Songs ♪ _____

📅 Birthday _____

🕐 Time _____

⚖ Weight _____

📏 Length _____

📍 Location _____

Headlines 📰 _____

World Leaders 🌍 _____

Watch Me Grow!

Lifting Head ___ Rolling Over ___ Sitting Up ___ Crawling ___ Pulling Up ___ Cruising ___ Walking ___

Firsts

Bath: _____

Smile: _____

Tooth: _____

Wave: _____

Slept Through
The Night: _____

Laugh: _____

My First Words: _____
_____

Nick Names
How and why
we chose name:

_____
_____
_____
_____
_____
_____
_____
_____
_____

Favorites

Toys: _____
_____
_____

Songs: _____
_____
_____

Books: _____
_____
_____

Likes: _____
_____

Dislikes: _____
_____

Look at My Growth

| 1 Month | Length: | Milestones: |
| | Weight: | |

| 2 Months | Length: | Milestones: |
| | Weight: | |

| 3 Months | Length: | Milestones: |
| | Weight: | |

| 4 Months | Length: | Milestones: |
| | Weight: | |

| 5 Months | Length: | Milestones: |
| | Weight: | |

| 6 Months | Length: | Milestones: |
| | Weight: | |

Then & Now

Birth

Hair: _____

Eye Color: _____

Length: _____

Weight: _____

1 Year

Hair: _____

Eye Color: _____

Length: _____

Weight: _____

| 7 Months | Length: | Milestones: |
| | Weight: | |

| 8 Months | Length: | Milestones: |
| | Weight: | |

| 9 Months | Length: | Milestones: |
| | Weight: | |

| 10 Months | Length: | Milestones: |
| | Weight: | |

| 11 Months | Length: | Milestones: |
| | Weight: | |

| 12 Months | Length: | Milestones: |
| | Weight: | |

Milestone Prompts
First Year

One Month
- Produces tears now when crying
- Moves head side-to-side while lying down
- Loves black and white or high contrast images

Two Months
- Plays with hands when sitting up but still flaps arms and legs when lying down
- Smiles intentionally

Three Months
- Giggling!
- Shows preference for one parent

Four Months
- Tastes salt now
- Beginning to play independently
- Rolls over (back to front)

Five Months
- Identifies parent's specific voice from a group of voices
- Reaches out for someone
- Shows stranger anxiety

Six Months
- Sits up with support
- Rolls over and back

Seven Months
- Imitates sounds
- Plays peek-a-boo

Eight Months
- Crawls
- Responds to name
- Sits unsupported
- Transfers objects between hands

Nine Months
- Waves "bye-bye"
- Drops toys then looks for them
- Identifies self in mirror

Ten Months
- Finger-feeds self
- Understands object permanence
- Pulls self to standing

Eleven Months
- Stands unsupported
- Prefers and responds more to repetitive sounds than non-repetitive sounds

Twelve Months
- Says "mama" or "dada"
- Brain has doubled in size
- Foot is half of its adult foot size

First Month

Second Month

Third Month

Fourth Month

Fifth Month

Sixth Month

Seventh Month

Eighth Month

Ninth Month

Tenth Month

Eleventh Month

Twelfth Month

Year Summary Prompts

- You are this tall
- Latest tricks
- Your pets or favorite animal
- Your favorite color
- Your favorite things to do
- Your favorite foods
- Your least favorite foods
- Your favorite drinks
- Your favorite friends
- Your favorite game
- Your favorite song
- Your favorite story book
- Your favorite toy
- Your favorite show
- Your favorite movie
- Your favorite holiday
- Your favorite place to go
- Something you do well
- 3 words to describe you
- You don't like to . . .
- You like to . . .
- You are happy when . . .
- A funny moment
- Funny sayings or expressions
- When you grow up you want to be

First Birthday

Who, when, and where we celebrated and who attended :

_____

_____

_____

_____

_____

_____

Second Birthday

Who, when, and where we celebrated and who attended :

_____

_____

_____

_____

_____

_____

Third Birthday

Who, when, and where we celebrated and who attended :

Fourth Birthday

Who, when, and where we celebrated and who attended :

_____

_____

_____

_____

_____

_____

Fifth Birthday

Who, when, and where we celebrated and who attended :

First Day of School

Date: _____ Your Age: _____

School Name: _____

Teacher's Name: _____

Location: _____

Memories and Photos: _____

_____

_____

_____

_____

_____

_____

Photos and Memories

_____
_____
_____
_____
_____
_____
_____
_____
_____
_____
_____

Photos and Memories

Photos and Memories

_____

_____

_____

_____

_____

_____

_____

_____

_____

_____

_____

Photos and Memories

_____

_____

_____

_____

_____

_____

_____

_____

_____

_____

_____

Photos and Memories

Photos and Memories

Made in the USA
Monee, IL
17 September 2021